Read & Respon

Ages
7-11

Read & Respond

Ages 7–11

Author: Eileen Jones

Commissioning Editor: Rachel Mackinnon

Development Editor: Rachel Coombs

Editor: Niamh O'Carroll

Assistant Editor: Caroline Carless

Series Designer: Anna Oliwa

Designer: Anna Oliwa

Illustrations: Mike Lacey, Beehive Illustration

Text © 2011 Eileen Jones © 2011 Scholastic Ltd

Designed using Adobe InDesign

Published by Scholastic Ltd,
Book End, Range Road, Witney,
Oxfordshire OX29 0YD
www.scholastic.co.uk

Printed by Bell & Bain
1 2 3 4 5 6 7 8 9   1 2 3 4 5 6 7 8 9 0

British Library Cataloguing-in-Publication Data
A catalogue record for this book is available from the British Library.

ISBN 978-1407-12626-5

Acknowledgements

The publishers gratefully acknowledge permission to reproduce the following copyright material: **Puffin Books** for the use of the cover from *The Railway Children* by E. Nesbit.
Every effort has been made to trace copyright holders for the works reproduced in this book, and the publishers apologise for any inadvertent omissions.

The Railway Children

About the book

The Railway Children is an established classic. Its elements of fantasy, mystery and adventure, but with serious lessons, make it ideal for upper Key Stage 2. It could be studied as a serialised class novel and there are links with many Literacy Framework genres: it is older literature, written by a significant author, and is set in a time of different traditions.

The book has more than one plot. In the first chapter, Father is dispatched to prison for spying, and Mother and the three children must live in poverty in a run-down house near a railway line. This main plot of a battle for justice is never forgotten but often recedes behind the story's day-to-day subplots. Mother is kept busy writing to earn money and the children, without school or adult supervision, enjoy considerable freedom. The railway's line, trains, station and staff, become the centre of their lives and many exploits.

The children experience exhilarating adventures, have ingenious ideas and find themselves in life-threatening situations. Relationships with the old gentleman and the Doctor confirm their trust in human nature; and friendships with the Porter, Station Master and Bargee teach them about very different lives. They gain insight into the pride of poor people and the importance of respect. Despite these thought-provoking lessons, this story was written to entertain children and is an adventure book of excitement and mystery.

In 1970, *The Railway Children* was made into a highly-acclaimed film. It has also been adapted for television numerous times and rewritten for the stage.

About the author

Edith Nesbit was born in London in 1858. She was a mischievous, tomboyish child, always looking for adventure. Nicknamed Daisy by her friends, she attended many schools but never settled and ran away more than once. Her sister had poor health, so the family moved frequently in the hope of finding a climate to suit her. They spent time in Brighton, Paris, Bordeaux, Spain and Germany before settling in Halstead, Kent. There, Edith spent happy childhood years, playing with her three brothers beside a railway.

As an adult, Edith remained a rebel, not acting as society expected women to: she dressed as she preferred and stated her opinion on a wide range of subjects. Nevertheless, she was sociable and popular.

Edith married Hubert Bland in 1880. She had begun writing in her teens, but it was not until Hubert became ill and his business partner swindled him that she, like Mother in the story, needed to take up writing seriously to earn money and her talent flourished. Her most successful book was *The Railway Children*, where the adventures Roberta, Peter and Phyllis enjoyed were probably influenced by Edith and her brothers' experiences, playing near the railway at their house in Kent. Edith Nesbit died in 1924.

Facts and figures

E. Nesbit wrote over 40 children's books, including: *The Story of the Treasure Seekers, The Wouldbegoods, Five Children and It* and *The Phoenix and the Carpet*.

She has been called 'the first modern writer for children'.

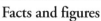

Guided reading

Chapter 1: The Beginning of Things

Talk about the function of openings: to hook the reader. In a long book, this is particularly important. Comment on pace, characters and social detail. Ask: *Do elements seem old-fashioned?* Refer to: vocabulary; servants; and class distinctions, particularly through characters' speech. Ask: *Do these take away from your enjoyment?* Suggest that the modern reader adapts, perceives modern views (*Girls are just as clever as boys*) and is attracted by the writer's friendly involvement, with *I* in the second sentence and the directly-addressed *You will think…*

Assess the chapter's success. Have the fast-moving plot, promising characters and mystery (Father's disappearance) hooked the reader?

Chapter 2: Peter's Coal-Mine

Point out *What fun!.* Investigate how life becomes fun. (Funny meals; the pump; the railway line, tunnel and station.) Comment on Roberta's remark *Better than toy-engines, isn't it?.* (Their new life is really exciting.)

Ask: *When does poverty stop being fun?* (Noticing that Mother is always busy; having either butter or jam; not lighting a fire when cold.) Debate the morality of Peter's 'mining'. Re-read his protestations to the Station Master, particularly *I was almost sure it wasn't.* Did he know that it was stealing? (Confirmation is in the chapter's final paragraph.)

Chapter 3: The Old Gentleman

Contrast their former street *where cabs and omnibuses rumbled by* and the country's *deep silence.* Point out the aside *I never saw a candlestick maker's cart, did you?* (Perhaps referring to the nursery rhyme's 'candlestick maker'.) Ask: *Where are the up trains going?* (Probably to London; hence the waves for Father.)

Explore character development. Peter behaves correctly, identifying himself to the Station Master, and apologising to the Porter about a tip. Bobbie empathises with Mother. Phyllis shows clumsy determination. (Her boots keep coming undone but she delivers the letter.) The children all display resourcefulness in meeting Mother's needs.

Refer to *untruly.* The Porter may be offended that a child friend suggests a tip.

Chapter 4: The Engine-Burglar

Identify period references: worry about the Doctor's bill and enjoyment of simple pleasures (flowers, the home-written song, games and limited presents of the birthday tea). Contrast them with today's National Health Service and more sophisticated celebrations. Would parents still react angrily to *telling everyone our affairs?*

Suggest that this chapter reveals most about Bobbie. Comment on awareness (Bobbie remembers Mother's feverish cry about the Doctor's bill and Mrs Viney's mention of a Club); problem-solving ability (she proposes a solution to the Doctor); and courage to act alone. Courage and generosity are evident when clambering into the cab to ask about Peter's engine.

Chapter 5: Prisoners and Captives

Suggest that lack of understanding causes fear and mistrust between the stranger and the crowd that surrounds him. Direct the children to the passage beginning *Sometimes, in moments of great need.* Sympathy for the man pushes Bobbie to communicate. Comment on her trust, smiling at the man and staying alone with him.

Consider Mother's knowledge and generosity. Point out Phyllis' comment *how very sorry you seem to be for him!.* Why is Mother silent and then mentions *all prisoners and captives?* (Perhaps she includes Father.)

Guided reading

Chapter 6: Saviours of the Train

Discuss character development, asking: *Is Perks offended? Why?* (No one visited with news, so now he carries on reading.) Refer to his hurt pride in Chapter 3. Talk about Phyllis: her dislike of ill-feeling; her way of making amends: *Oh, let's kiss and be friends*, and her honesty about the strawberries.

Ask: *Who takes charge after the landslide?* Suggest that Peter starts thinking immediately, leads and makes business-like decisions, but Bobbie acts with independent courage. Refer to the chapter's last line. It implies that the writer and reader, unlike *The others*, understand Bobbie.

Chapter 7: For Valour

Let the children re-read the first two paragraphs. Ask: *Which characteristics are praised?* (Wanting to make others happy; keeping secrets; *silent sympathy*.) *How does Bobbie 'help lame dogs over stiles'?* (She supports Mother and the Russian gentleman.) *What do Bobbie's dreams reveal?* (Shock, horror and pride.)

Point out Mother's instruction to refuse money. Ask: *Is Mother sensitive about their poverty?* Suggest that she may consider accepting money inappropriate. Remark on Peter being pushed forward to make a speech. Is this a male role? Explore the old gentleman's visit and question why *Bobbie crept away.* (Is she emotional herself?) Point out her observation of Mother's fatigue and hand tightening. Ask: *Why did she start a race she hated?* (To distract Phyllis and leave Mother to think.)

Chapter 8: The Amateur Fireman

Point out *the dearest friend.* Ask: *Are you surprised? How do the children want to show their affection?* (Celebrating Perks' birthday.) Investigate the initial Bargee encounter, noting the Bargee's

agressive behaviour, Peter's righteous self-confidence and the girls' loyalty.

Examine initial reactions to the fire: Peter is unconcerned; Phyllis thinks of the dog; Bobbie, maturely, remembers the baby. Why is Peter *staggering*? (Smoke, the baby and wet clothes.) Comment on Bobbie's physical and mental strength: she runs *like the wind* and interrupts the party of bargees. Discuss the writer's message: other groups may form *pleasant society*. Bill is recognised as *nice as anyone*; the children are accepted as the *real, right sort*.

Chapter 9: The Pride of Perks

Why does Mother correct 'kids' and 'missus'? (This is not good, correct English.) *Who is Bobbie repeating?* (Perks.) Point out Mother's further correction with *anticipate*. Ask: *Does this make Bobbie seem like you?* Notice that the children collect without Mother's permission. Ask: *Would she approve?* (She might view it as begging or mention Perks' pride.) Ask: *Why does Mrs Ransome give the gooseberries?* (Her birthday has been celebrated.) Analyse Mother's words: her emphasis on *how*, her understanding *that poor people are very proud*, their dislike of *charity*. Define *charity*.

What is Perks' *pet particular*? (Probably his favourite tobacco.) Ask: *Why is Perks horrified by the gifts?* (He fears *charity*.) *What does he realise?* (The gifts are given out of respect.)

Chapter 10: The Terrible Secret

Assess the importance of Mother and Bobbie's conversation: Mother is reassured that Father is remembered, Bobbie that Mother appreciates their efforts to be good. Investigate the rake accident and debate the blame. Ask: *When does Bobbie probably become worried?* (When Peter faints and she sees the injury.) Point out *Phyllis was halfway to the Doctor's.* Comment on Phyllis' minor role, following the lead or mediating in disagreements.

Guided reading

Analyse Bobbie's remorse and worry about Peter's future. Divide the class into boys and girls for a reading of their peace-making conversation. Afterwards ask: *Was your speech old-fashioned? Were words strange?* Emphasise the significance of the newspaper: Bobbie discovers what the trouble is.

Chapter 11: The Hound in the Red Jersey

Suggest that Bobbie, sharing the secret with Mother, needs greater maturity. Ask: *Are you surprised by her initiative in writing to the old gentleman?* (She has already shown initiative in her suggestion to the Doctor about the *Club*.) Contrast Bobbie and Peter's determination to wait for the red-jerseyed boy, with Phyllis' babyish talk of hunger. Point out how knowledgeable the older children are, ready for a train in the tunnel. Identify Peter's struggle to be courageous: *caught hold of Bobbie's arm; trembled; before he could speak in his natural voice.*

Discuss the chapter's ending. Suggest that it is more of a 'cliffhanger' than usual, the incident is incomplete.

Chapter 12: What Bobbie Brought Home

Identify textual evidence of Bobbie struggling with herself to show courage in the tunnel. She fights claustrophobic panic in *Don't be a silly little girl*, and battles fainting at the sight of the boy's leg in *Silly little girl*.

Peter later shows courage as he indignantly rejects the signalman's bribe. Ask: *Are you surprised that Phyllis, who usually likes everyone, calls him a nasty man? Does she later revert to character?* (She says *Kiss and be friends*.)

Chapter 13: The Hound's Grandfather

Ask: *Would the local doctor set Jim's leg nowadays?* (Jim would attend hospital.) Investigate the children's behaviour, suggesting that play is a relief after frightening reality. What is the Doctor's reaction? Point out *cheerfully*, emphasising Phyllis' innocence. Peter did not intend the game to happen (*I had to go through with it*) and refuses to let Bobbie be blamed. Explore the Doctor's advice to Peter. (Girls and women are easily hurt by words.) How does Peter react? Notice Bobbie's understanding as they struggle to make peace: *he's sorry, really, only he won't say so.*

Re-read Peter and Mother's conversation, identifying what he misses. (Male company and school.) *Why must he wait another year?* (The expense.) Discuss how characters and storylines meet in Jim's grandfather. *Which private word lights up Bobbie's face?* (Hope.)

Chapter 14: The End

Aspects of previous life return with a cook, a housemaid and an end to paid writing. Ask: *What do the children gain?* (They stop housework and Mother composes rhymes again.) *Are there disadvantages?* (Lessons and little time for the railway.)

Point out fairytale elements, Bobbie saying *I wish something would happen*. Investigate the events: the old gentleman's organisation of passengers; newspapers open at *one certain part*; Bobbie's instinctive *something was going to happen!*

Question why Bobbie meets the train alone. (She has known the secret.) Point out Father's appreciative *she told me what you'd been to her.* Debate the writer's decision to give the family privacy from the reader. Is it a successful ending?

Shared reading

Extract 1

- This extract from the opening pages introduces characters, sets the scene and begins the action.
- Underline the sentence beginning *Of course...* Whose opinion is this about Mother? (The writer's.) Discuss whether this reveals the writer's preference for Roberta.
- Underline *who meant very well.* What is implied? (Although well-intentioned, Phyllis is not very capable.)
- Read the first sentence of paragraph two. What custom is referred to? (Paying calls was customary for ladies in such houses at this time.)

Ask: *Which words reveal the writer's view of the custom?* (*dully* and *dull*.)
- Read paragraph three. Which adjectives depict an idyllic life? Circle: *lucky, pretty, good, lovely, kind, merry, perfect.* Question why the writer makes life almost too ideal. (To build atmosphere ready for a contrast.)
- Comment on the final paragraph's brevity. Which phrase has impact? Circle *dreadful change.* How are the story and reader affected? (Mystery is introduced and the reader wants to continue.)

Extract 2

- In this extract the children use homemade red flags to warn of the blocked railway line.
- Circle *suspense.* What does it mean here? (Waiting with dread.)
- Read as far as *would be killed.* Are these the writer's thoughts? (Bobbie's. Underline *It seemed to her.*) Does the increasing negativity match Bobbie's growing panic?
- In paragraph three, circle exclamation marks suggesting tone and volume. Let the class take turns reading Peter's speech aloud. Ask: *Were his instructions clear? What helped?* (Brief, clear

directions, uncluttered clauses and precise language: *big furze, on.*)
- Use highlighting to track Bobbie's physical state: *feel sick; cold and trembled; could hardly hold; did not tremble now.*
- Read from *It seemed* to the end. Circle *fiercely* and *suddenly,* emphasising that Peter exerts control. Underline *dragged Phyllis back.* What does this show? (His sense of responsibility and awareness of Phyllis' ignorance.)
- Ask: *Who controls Bobbie?* (She decides herself to keep waving the flags.) *Is she courageous?*

Extract 3

- This extract is from the final pages as Father, unannounced to the family, returns.
- Read aloud Perks' speech. Discuss tense, grammar and pronunciation. Question why the writer ascribes mistakes to Perks and servants. (They are presented as lower class and poorly-educated.) Class divisions were far more distinct then.
- Underline the first sentence of paragraph four. Who is the writer addressing? (The reader.) Ask: *Is the reader likely to guess?* Emphasise the distinction between Bobbie's heart and mind. Which is expectant? (Highlight *heart* and *expectant* in the

same colour.) Which is *almost blank?* (Highlight *mind* and *almost blank* in a new colour.)
- Read paragraph five. Comment on the everyday scene. Circle the dash. What does it suggest? (Interruption.) Examine punctuation in paragraph six's first sentence, circling exclamation marks. What do they suggest? (Sudden, loud speech.)
- Underline *like a knife.* What device has the writer used? (Simile.) How is it effective? (Bobbie's words penetrate people's emotions.) What does the final sentence emphasise? (Difference, but unity.) Circle *tall, little, clinging, tightly.*

Extract 1

From Chapter 1 'The Beginning of Things'

There were three of them. Roberta was the eldest. Of course, Mothers never have favourites, but if their Mother *had* had a favourite, it might have been Roberta. Next came Peter, who wished to be an Engineer when he grew up; and the youngest was Phyllis, who meant extremely well.

Mother did not spend all her time in paying dull calls to dull ladies, and sitting dully at home waiting for dull ladies to pay calls to her. She was almost always there, ready to play with the children, and read to them, and help them to do their home-lessons. Besides this she used to write stories for them while they were at school, and read them aloud after tea, and she always made up funny pieces of poetry for their birthdays and for other great occasions, such as the christening of the new kittens, or the refurnishing of the doll's house, or the time when they were getting over the mumps.

These three lucky children always had everything they needed: pretty clothes, good fires, a lovely nursery with heaps of toys, and a Mother Goose wallpaper. They had a kind and merry nursemaid, and a dog who was called James, and who was their very own. They also had a Father who was just perfect – never cross, never unjust, and always ready for a game – at least, if at any time he was *not* ready, he always had an excellent reason for it, and explained the reason to the children so interestingly and funnily that they felt sure he couldn't help himself.

You will think that they ought to have been very happy. And so they were, but they did not know *how* happy till the pretty life in Edgecombe Villa was over and done with, and they had to live a very different life indeed.

The dreadful change came quite suddenly.

Text by E. Nesbit.

Extract 2

From Chapter 6 'Saviours of the Train'

And Bobbie began to feel sick with suspense.

It seemed to her that they had been standing there for hours and hours, holding those silly little red flannel flags that no one would ever notice. The train wouldn't care. It would go rushing by them and tear round the corner and go crashing into that awful mound. And everyone would be killed. Her hands grew very cold and trembled so that she could hardly hold the flag. And then came the distant rumble and hum of the metals, and a puff of white steam showed far away along the stretch of line.

'Stand firm,' said Peter, 'and wave like mad! When it gets to that big furze bush step back, but go on waving! Don't stand *on* the line, Bobbie!'

The train came rattling along very, very fast.

'They don't see us! They won't see us! It's all no good!' cried Bobbie.

The two little flags on the line swayed as the nearing train shook and loosened the heaps of loose stones that held them up. One of them slowly leaned over and fell on the line. Bobbie jumped forward and caught it up, and waved it; her hands did not tremble now.

It seemed that the train came on as fast as ever. It was very near now.

'Keep off the line, you silly cuckoo!' said Peter, fiercely.

'It's no good,' Bobbie said again.

'Stand back!' cried Peter, suddenly, and he dragged Phyllis back by the arm.

But Bobbie cried, 'Not yet, not yet!' and waved her two flags right over the line.

Text by E. Nesbit.

Extract 3

From Chapter 14 'The End'

'Like this 'ere!' said Perks. 'Don't I tell you I see it in the paper?'

'Saw *what* in the paper?' asked Bobbie, but already the 11.54 was steaming into the station and the Station Master was looking at all the places where Perks was not and ought to have been.

Bobbie was left standing alone, the Station Cat watching her from under the bench with friendly golden eyes.

Of course you know already exactly what was going to happen. Bobbie was not so clever. She had the vague, confused, expectant feeling that comes to one's heart in dreams. What her heart expected I can't tell – perhaps the very thing that you and I know was going to happen – but her mind expected nothing; it was almost blank, and felt nothing but tiredness and stupidness and an empty feeling like your body has when you have been for a long walk and it is very far indeed past your proper dinner-time.

Only three people got out of the 11.54. The first was a countrywoman with two baskety boxes full of live chickens who stuck their russet heads out anxiously through the wicker bars; the second was Miss Peckitt, the grocer's wife's cousin, with a tin box and three brown-paper parcels; and the third –

'Oh! my Daddy, my Daddy!' That scream went like a knife into the heart of everyone in the train, and people put their heads out of the windows to see a tall pale man with lips set in a thin close line, and a little girl clinging to him with arms and legs, while his arms went tightly round her.

Text by E. Nesbit.

Plot, character and setting

Understanding the writer

> **Objective:** To infer writers' perspectives from what is written and what is implied.
> **What you need:** Copies of *The Railway Children*, photocopiable page 15, writing materials.
> **Cross-curricular link:** History.

What to do

● After reading Chapter 1, explain that views differed from today in 1906. Suggest that the author implies her views through characters or vocabulary. Revise the difference between explicit (stated) and implicit information (inferred or suggested).

● Ask: *What female social custom is mentioned?* (Ladies paying calls.) What opinion does the writer imply? (She thinks it dull.) Give out photocopiable page 15 for the children to complete the first section.

● Identify *Mothers never have favourites* near the beginning. Ask: *What is implied about Nesbit's belief?* (Mothers should love their children equally.) Ask about Mother's personality, involvement with the children, and response to difficulty. (Brave strength.) Suggest that, through the character of Mother, Nesbit suggests her own expectations of mothers.

● Refer to Father's after-dinner talk. Ask: *Is this Nesbit's view on gender equality?* Read aloud the example of Ruth's poor grammar. Ask: *Does Nesbit view servants as uneducated?*

● Let the children complete the photocopiable sheet, referring to or quoting the text.

> **Differentiation**
> **For older/more confident learners:** Ask children to find more than one textual reference for some subjects.
> **For younger/less confident learners:** Encourage partner discussion, direct them to textual evidence and accept shorter answers.

Keeping a journal

> **Objective:** To sustain engagement with longer texts, using different techniques to make the text come alive.
> **What you need:** Copies of *The Railway Children*, photocopiable page 16, a new exercise book for each child, writing materials, internet access to paintings and music (optional).

What to do

● After reading Chapter 1, advise the children that this long story may be complicated. Suggest using a journal to keep track of the story and help to stay interested in it.

● Hold partner, then class, discussions about information to include: events since the last journal entry; character development; points of interest; dates and places mentioned; unusual language; personal response; predictions.

● Propose regular journal entries. Advise following a format, so that chapters of character development or adventure are obvious.

● Display the headings from photocopiable page 16. Organise paired, then class, discussion relating Chapter 1 to each heading. Encourage personal reactions to the book.

● For the final section, talk about varied media forms. Children may express their response to the chapter with an illustration, poster or cartoon, or may suggest a well-known painting or piece of music.

● Give everyone photocopiable page 16 and a journal exercise book. Suggest using a double-page spread each time, using the photocopiable sheet as a template for future entries.

> **Differentiation**
> **For older/more confident learners:** Encourage longer entries and wider variation and research for supporting art forms.
> **For younger/less confident learners:** Let partners work together, but encourage a personal reaction to the story.

Plot, character and setting

Character traits

> **Objective:** To make notes on and use evidence from across a text to explain events or ideas.
> **What you need:** Copies of *The Railway Children*, photocopiable page 17, writing materials.
> **Cross-curricular link:** PSHE.

What to do
● After finishing Chapter 4, propose identifying the character traits of the three railway children.
● Direct the children to scan Chapters 1 and 2 and consider Roberta's behaviour. Can they describe her in one adjective? (Observant; thoughtful.) Ask them to write down their chosen adjective and note textual proof. Let talk-partners share ideas. Do they agree with the other's choice? Choose children to report to the class.
● Display photocopiable page 17. Explain that partners will scan the text as far as the end of Chapter 4. Considering a character's behaviour, they must apply appropriate adjectives.

● Each pair will work with two copies of the photocopiable sheet. On one copy, they must write their adjectives in the character's word boxes. In the same locations on the second copy, they will note brief textual evidence.
● Give each pair two copies of the photocopiable sheet. Suggest aiming at five adjectives for each character, but advise that some characters may reveal fewer traits.

> **Differentiation**
> **For older/more confident learners:** Let children work independently and provide more detailed textual explanation in notes of their own format.
> **For younger/less confident learners:** Encourage the children to work on one chapter at a time, choosing an adjective for each character. Assist with a bank of adjectives.

Pictures in words

> **Objective:** To explore how writers use language for dramatic effect.
> **What you need:** Copies of *The Railway Children*, writing materials.
> **Cross-curricular link:** Geography.

What to do
● Suggest that Chapter 6's landslide is one of the most dramatic incidents so far. With no illustration, the writer relies on using effective language.
● Ask the children to fold a piece of paper into four storyboard squares with these headings: 1. 'The occasion'; 2. 'The cutting'; 3. 'Noise and movement'; 4. 'The landslide'.
● Read the section in Chapter 6 from *And this idea* to *And they started*. Ask: *What is revealed about the occasion?* (The children go in search of wild cherries.) *What physical details are given?* (Trees and their blossom.) *Which language is effective?* (*Rocky*; the simile comparing cherry

blossom to snow and silver.) Ask the children to record what the reader learns and which language helps in the first square.
● Write on the whiteboard where the remaining sections end (continuing on from *And they started*): 2. *rabbit's grave*; 3. *railway was enchanted*; 4. *A cloud of dust rose up.*
● Advise partners to read and discuss one section at a time before writing independently in the storyboard square. Revise personification, similes, and onomatopoeia. Remind them to explain the information given and to give examples of effective language.

> **Differentiation**
> **For older/more confident learners:** Ask children to repeat the exercise for Chapter 1's train journey and the arrival at the house.
> **For younger/less confident learners:** Encourage greater partner collaboration and accept less writing.

Plot, character and setting

Back in time

> **Objective:** To compare how writers from different times and places present experiences and use language.
> **What you need:** Copies of *The Railway Children*, writing materials, individual whiteboards.
> **Cross-curricular link:** History.

What to do
● After reading Chapter 7, ask: *Have you noticed a reference to the period of the book?* Point out 1905 engraved on the watches presented to the railway children. Ask: *Does the date surprise you? Did you realise the book was set so long ago?*
● Comment on steam trains. Ask: *Why are the children so relaxed about being near railway lines?* (There is no electricity in the lines.)
● Invite talk-partners to discuss which aspects of the text reveal a setting of 1905. Ask them to write an appropriate heading for one aspect on their whiteboards. Let the children show their boards and compare words. Agree on and display these headings: 'Clothes'; 'Speech'; 'Goods'; 'Names'; 'Machines'; 'Behaviour'.
● Suggest the children divide their page into six squares with these headings. Encourage them, independently or with a partner, to search for evidence in Chapters 2, 4 and 7 and write the examples in the squares.
● Share and discuss the results, debating modern-day replacements. Make a class display of interesting evidence that this story is set in the early 20th century.

> **Differentiation**
> **For older/more confident learners:** Let children scan all the chapters read so far.
> **For younger/less confident learners:** Encourage partner collaboration on every part of the task, and suggest working on only Chapters 2 and 7.

Good intentions

> **Objective:** To understand underlying themes, causes and points of view.
> **What you need:** Copies of *The Railway Children*, photocopiable page 18, writing materials.
> **Cross-curricular link:** PSHE.

What to do
● Read together the final paragraph of Chapter 9. Draw attention to *one has to be careful to do it in the right way* and Perks' comment that *it's not so much what you do, as what you mean.* Suggest that Nesbit is expressing her moral code: good intentions and correct behaviour bring good results. Explain that this proves true in many of the book's incidents. (For example, asking the old gentleman for things when Mother is ill.)
● Revise the 'coal mining' incident from Chapter 2. Ask: *What is Peter's good intention?* (To provide coal for the family.) *What happens?* (The Station Master is angry.) *How, in Chapter 3, does Peter behave correctly?* (He admits his identity to the Station Master.) *What is the good ending?* (An invitation to the station.)
● Give photocopiable page 18 to each child, for them to complete the sections about Peter's coal mining.
● Refer the children to Chapters 3, 4 and 9 to scan the incidents: the children ask the old gentleman for a parcel; Bobbie climbs into the engine; they ask villagers for gifts. Invite paired discussion; then the children can complete the photocopiable sheet to show evidence of Nesbit's moral code.

> **Differentiation**
> **For older/more confident learners:** Let children investigate other incidents: Bobbie's proposal to the Doctor; the barge rescue; approaching the Russian gentleman.
> **For younger/less confident learners:** Encourage partner collaboration and guide scanning; ask for oral answers first.

Plot, character and setting

The passage of time

> **Objective:** To compare different types of narrative texts and identify how they are structured.
> **What you need:** Copies of *The Railway Children*, writing materials.
> **Cross-curricular link:** History.

What to do

● After finishing the book, suggest that time is important to its plot and structure. Challenge talk-partners to tell each other how much time elapses between the book's start and finish.

● Invite partners to scan Chapter 1, identifying the annual occasion marked. (Peter's birthday.) Ask: *When is another family birthday celebrated?* (Roberta's birthday in Chapter 4.) *What suggests that the story covers less than a year?* (There is no mention of another one for Peter.)

● Direct the children to scan Chapters 2 and 14. Which months are mentioned? (May and September.) Ask: *What would normally occupy*

a lot of this time for children? What is different here? (The railway children do not go to school.) Let the children write their answers before comparing results.

● Can the children find a mention of school in Chapter 1? Ask: *Is there a reference in the final chapters?* (Peter and Mother's conversation in Chapter 13.)

● Ask for a written paragraph about how absence from school affects the railway children. Does it affect their time? Is it important to the story's events? (Long, free days allow involvement in numerous incidents.)

> **Differentiation**
> **For older/more confident learners:** Encourage longer answers and an investigation of how free time matters to them.
> **For younger/less confident learners:** Allow paired work on one question at a time.

Connecting themes

> **Objective:** To understand underlying themes, causes and points of view.
> **What you need:** Copies of *The Railway Children*, writing materials.
> **Cross-curricular link:** PSHE.

What to do

● Use this activity after completing the whole book. Pose questions to talk-partners before commencing whole-class exchanges.

● Point out the first sentence's connection to the title, confirming the main characters. Ask: *Which child is most important?*

● Suggest that Phyllis, a follower and appeaser, receives least attention.

● Discuss Peter: his love of adventure, determination to win arguments and desire to be in charge and take credit for ideas.

● Analyse Bobbie's kindness, sensitivity, independence, resourcefulness and increasing maturity. Consider Nesbit's inferred preference

on the first page: *If their Mother had had a favourite, it might have been Roberta.*

● Ask the children to list: 1. the three children; 2. the adults in the story. Using a different colour for each child, suggest drawing links to the adults to represent private meetings or arrangements.

● Display your version. Emphasise Bobbie's links: nursing Mother; dealings with the Doctor and old gentleman; calming the Russian; sharing Mother's secret; welcoming Father.

● Conclude that Bobbie connects the book's themes: adult mysteries and children's adventures. Hence, Bobbie is the main character.

> **Differentiation**
> **For older/more confident learners:** Expect deeper character analysis and more perceptive comments.
> **For younger/less confident learners:** Invite paired investigation. Advise which chapters to scan.

Understanding the writer

- What does the writer imply about her own views? Complete the table with references to the text.

The subject	What the writer implies	Textual evidence
Social customs (the author's thoughts about how ladies occupy themselves at home)		
Mothers (the author's thoughts about how mothers should behave)		
Servants (the author's thoughts about servants' educational standards and status)		
Distinctions between boys and girls (the author's thoughts about expectations of boys and girls)		

SECTION
4

Keeping a journal

● Complete your journal entry for the chapter you have read today.

Date _____

Stage of story reached _____

What has happened since the last entry?

_____

_____

_____

Character developments	Mystery or adventure
_____	_____
_____	_____
_____	_____
Time and place references	**Special vocabulary**
_____	_____
_____	_____

My reaction to the story _____

_____

What I think will happen next _____

_____

_____

My idea for a supporting art form for this section.
(Recommend a famous painting or piece of music to suit this section.
Alternatively, add your own illustration on a facing page.)

_____

_____

Illustration © 2011, Mike Lacey, Beehive Illustration.

SCHOLASTIC
www.scholastic.co.uk

Character traits

● Write adjectives to describe the character traits shown in Chapters 1 to 4.

Bobbie

Peter

Phyllis

Good intentions

● Complete the table below by adding evidence from the text to support the belief that the children's good intentions and behaviour lead to happy endings.

What the children do	Good intentions and methods	Happy endings
Peter goes coal mining		
They ask the old gentleman for a parcel		
Bobbie climbs into the engine		
They ask villagers for gifts		

■SCHOLASTIC
www.scholastic.co.uk

READ & RESPOND: Activities based on The Railway Children

Talk about it

What a story!

> **Objective:** To tell a story using notes designed to cue techniques such as repetition, recap and humour.
> **What you need:** Copies of *The Railway Children*, photocopiable page 22, writing materials.
> **Cross-curricular link:** Drama.

What to do
● Put the children into pairs to scan and discuss Chapter 5: the platform confusion; communication problems; the foreign stranger at Three Chimneys; his history (authorship of a book about poor Russians; imprisonment; banishment to Siberia; a soldier; escape).
● Suggest that Perks will want to know everything. Set a scenario: the children visit the Porters' Room to relate the story.
● Let the children decide individually which storyteller to be: Bobbie or Peter. As storytellers, they must organise facts, including their own feelings. Emphasise telling, not reading, a story.

Use talk-partners before discussing techniques for keeping listeners engaged as a class. (Repetition, recap and humour.)
● Give the children photocopiable page 22 to write cue cards. These will be prompts containing brief notes and reminders of techniques to use to keep Perks engaged.
● Once ready, let the children practise their storytelling on partners. Progress to groups, so everyone experiences speaking to a group.
● Encourage listeners to become Perks, rating how well they understand the story and how well their interest is held.

> **Differentiation**
> **For older/more confident learners:** Ask children to tell their story to the class, or as Phyllis.
> **For younger/less confident learners:** Reduce writing and the number of cue cards. Limit storytelling to small groups.

Adding dialogue

> **Objective:** To perform a scripted scene, making use of dramatic conventions.
> **What you need:** Copies of *The Railway Children*, writing materials.
> **Cross-curricular link:** Drama.

What to do
● After Chapter 7, comment that this book is often subtly funny. Focus on the scene when the children go to the station to speak to the old gentleman. Point out Bobbie's amusing hope that he will not notice Phyllis behind the other two because *The aged are often weak in the eyes.*
● Investigate the following pages. Ask: *What is Bobbie's funny vocabulary mistake?* (*Direction* instead of 'director'.) *How does the old gentleman play with language?* (*Fryingpansky.*)
● Put the children into groups of four. Point out the writer's summary in the waiting-room scene: *…a great deal more.* Suggest supplying this missing dialogue. Encourage the groups to

first read from the start of the scene to *Tell me all about yourself* to become used to the speech style, and intentional and unintentional humour.
● Let the groups work on the dialogue, amending Phyllis' part so that she is involved. Encourage improvised dialogue before the children write their playscript and stage directions. Recommend using computers to make writing and editing easier. Remind them to use subtle humour.
● Finish with each group assessing another group's scripted performance.

> **Differentiation**
> **For older/more confident learners:** Ask children to write dialogue for the railway children's walk home later.
> **For younger/less confident learners:** Limit dialogue to two pieces of speech for each character. Suggest words that Peter and Bobbie could amusingly muddle up.

Talk about it

Personal dilemmas

> **Objective:** To improvise using a range of drama strategies and conventions to explore themes such as hopes, fears and desires.
> **What you need:** Copies of *The Railway Children*, writing materials.
> **Cross-curricular link:** PSHE.

What to do

● After Chapter 10, comment that Bobbie is a good, not bad, character. Nevertheless, enthusiasm for adventure is a weakness affecting her decisions.

● Consider Chapter 2's coal-mining incident: although Bobbie realises that Peter is stealing coal, she does not tell Mother and helps to cart coal to the house.

● Divide the class into two groups: Group A representing Bobbie's good side, Group B her bad side. Ask Group A to think of comments to stop Bobbie helping Peter to steal coal. Group B should think of remarks to encourage her.

● Arrange the two groups in facing parallel lines. As Bobbie, walk slowly down the 'alley' between the lines, the children speaking their lines as you near them. Having listened to your conscience (their voices), make your decision.

● Choose children to play Bobbie and walk through the alley. Does every Bobbie reach the same decision? Use new conscience alleys to examine Bobbie's decision to ask villagers for gifts for Perks without Mother's prior permission; and investigate her argumentative nature in the rake dispute.

● Create smaller alleys so more children experience listening to their conscience.

> **Differentiation**
> **For older/more confident learners:** Ask children to plan a conscience alley for Peter.
> **For younger/less confident learners:** Let partners practise comments, and speak together if preferred.

Catch the moment

> **Objective:** To consider the overall impact of a live or recorded performance, identifying dramatic ways of conveying characters' ideas and building tension.
> **What you need:** Copies of *The Railway Children*, photocopiable page 23, writing materials.
> **Cross-curricular link:** Drama.

What to do

● After Chapter 12, suggest that photographs of the story's dramatic moments would reveal much about the characters' feelings. Explain the term 'freeze-frame', in which children create a silent tableau of characters at a moment in the story.

● Arrange the children into groups of five. Give each group a card from photocopiable page 23. Encourage collaborative decision-making to allocate roles, consult text and rehearse a freeze-frame.

● As each group presents a freeze-frame to the rest of the class, does the audience recognise the moment? Let individual characters step out of the tableau and speak their thoughts.

● For other characters, use thought-tracking: invite a member of the audience to stand next to the frozen character and speak their thoughts aloud. Ask: *How will you know what to say?* (Characters' facial expressions and body language reveal some of their thoughts.)

● Finish with the groups exchanging cards and repeating the activity, this time with more expressive facial expressions and body language.

> **Differentiation**
> **For older/more confident learners:** Children could create another freeze-frame for their card, departing from the story or changing a character's personality or reaction, and hence their thoughts.
> **For younger/less confident learners:** Move among groups, offering support and ideas. Whisper prompts for their spoken thoughts.

Talk about it

Making decisions

> **Objective:** To understand the process of decision making.
> **What you need:** Copies of *The Railway Children*, writing materials.
> **Cross-curricular link:** PSHE.

What to do
● After Chapter 12, return to Peter's discovery of the sleeping signalman. Ask: *What will happen if the signalman is reported?* (He may lose his job. The children may be unwelcome at the station.) Emphasise the importance of who finds him asleep and their decision.
● Put the children into pairs, one as the signalman and one as Peter. Let partners improvise dialogue for one to two minutes.
● Signal the children to stop. Leave one pair in character as the other children and question them about their feelings. Ask Peter: *What concerns you?* (The signalman broke railway rules.)
● Invite the pairs to repeat the exercise with the signalman being found by Phyllis and partners exchanging the role of the signalman. Hot-seat a new pair for the children to question. Continue in this way, with discovery by Mrs Viney and finally Mother. Ask Mrs Viney: *What about his family?* (She may know his dependants.) Ask Mother: *Is he responsible enough?* (Mother may talk about a duty to society.)
● Divide the class into groups of four to discuss what they have heard from the hot-seating and their own conversations. Do they want to report the signalman? Share conclusions.

> **Differentiation**
> **For older/more confident learners:** Ask children to use paired improvisation for a decision-making meeting between Mother and Peter after discovering the sleeping signalman.
> **For younger/less confident learners:** Provide useful conversation openers.

Adventure or mystery?

> **Objective:** To participate in whole-class debate, using the conventions and language of debate, including standard English.
> **What you need:** Copies of *The Railway Children*, photocopiable page 24, writing materials.
> **Cross-curricular link:** Citizenship.

What to do
● After completing the book, admit that you have yet to decide on its library category. Ask for the children's help to decide whether it should be classed as 'Adventure' or 'Mystery'.
● Give out photocopiable page 24. Explain that the children must prepare an oral case for both categories. Suggest writing notes, listing three or four arguments for each category, and convincing phrases to say.
● Remind the children to be ready to back up a point with evidence by referring to the plot. Point out that the plot references around the page may be useful, but the children may choose better ones of their own.
● Once the children have completed their notes, divide the class into two groups, assigning the support of one category to each group. Chair the debate formally, listening to arguments from both sides. Limit speaking time so that everyone contributes.
● Sum up the arguments you have heard. Encourage the children to listen carefully to help them make up their minds. Give the children a 'free' vote as individuals, not as part of a group.

> **Differentiation**
> **For older/more confident learners:** Ask children to prepare a case for the 'Historical fiction' category.
> **For younger/less confident learners:** Let children work in pairs, or prepare the case for just one category.

Talk about it

What a story!

● Cut out the cards and make notes to use as prompts to help you to tell Perks all about the Russian gentleman.

1. Commotion at the station What did you think about the crowd and the stranger? Were you excited? Storytelling technique:	**2. Communication problems** Did you speak to the foreign stranger? Were you pleased with yourself? Storytelling technique:
3. Taking him to Three Chimneys How did you feel about having him there? Were you sympathetic? Storytelling technique:	**4. Learning about his history** What nationality is he? Is he a good man? Storytelling technique:
5. Why he is in this country What does he want to do? Is he likely to succeed? Storytelling technique:	**6. Now** How will you try to help him? Storytelling technique:

Catch the moment

● Cut out the cards and create freeze-frames of key story moments from *The Railway Children.*

Mother and the three children have arrived for the first time at Three Chimneys. A candle lights up the large, bare kitchen. The cart man carries in their boxes.	Bobbie has run to the 'Rose and Crown'. Barge people are drinking beer and talking. She calls out for Bill the Bargeman to tell him about the fire.
A foreign stranger is on the railway platform. He has pushed the Station Master away. The other children stand back as Bobbie speaks French to him.	A birthday tea is laid out and presents for Mr Perks are in a pram. Mr and Mrs Perks are arguing about the presents. The children listen from behind the wash-house door.
The other children have been presented with watches. The Station Master has pushed Peter forward to make a speech to the group of people sitting and watching.	Roberta is in the tunnel with the injured red-jerseyed boy. Peter and Phyllis have discovered the signalman asleep in a chair. Peter shouts at him to wake up.

Talk about it

Adventure or mystery?

● Using the events provided as inspiration, write notes and persuasive phrases in favour of categorising the book as each genre.

The children's red flags stop the train.	Mother does not talk about Father's disappearance.	A stranger speaking an unknown language arrives.	Bobbie rides in the engine-driver's cab.

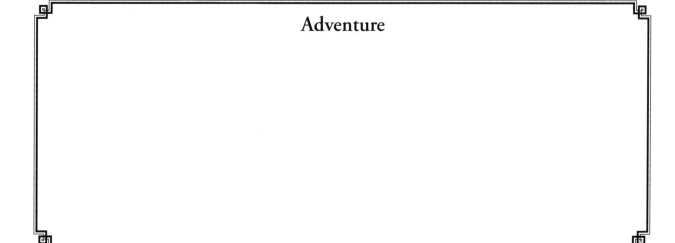

Adventure

Mystery

The old gentleman gives gifts to strange children.	The Russian gentleman's family are missing.	Peter mines and transports coal from the station.	The children rescue a baby from a barge.

Get writing

Mood poetry

> **Objective:** To use different narrative techniques to engage and entertain the reader.
> **What you need:** Copies of *The Railway Children*, photocopiable page 28, writing materials.
> **Cross-curricular link:** PSHE.

What to do

● After reading Chapter 1, comment on progression: early idyllic scenes; minor upset of the model Engine; surprise and concern at visitors; bewildering changes; a dramatic move.

● Suggest that the writer's narrative style also progresses: a happy, friendly tone in the early pages; humorous rhyme about the Engine; tense speech with the visit; harsh descriptions and unhappy dialogue for the changes (life is horrid and meals dull and dirty); strong, negative vocabulary for the move (*melancholy, unhappy, hammered*).

● Identify Mother's attempts at reassurance: *It'll all come right in the end* and, on the evening before the move, she laughs at Peter's wish to move once a month. Suggest that Mother needs a new poem now to make Roberta less anxious.

● Propose that the children write Mother's poem. Ask: *What should the subject be?* (The move.) *What mood?* (Light-hearted and confident.) Read together Mother's earlier poem. Analyse content, construction and language. Point out: the storytelling style; rhyme pattern; accurate and perceptive vocabulary; light tone.

● Give out photocopiable page 28. Suggest first sharing ideas with a partner, trying out lines orally and making preliminary drafts.

> **Differentiation**
> **For older/more confident learners:** Suggest writing a second poem for their arrival at the new house.
> **For younger/less confident learners:** Let partners collaborate on their poem.

Exchanging letters

> **Objective:** To adapt sentence construction to different text types, purposes and readers.
> **What you need:** Copies of *The Railway Children*, writing materials.
> **Cross-curricular link:** History.

What to do

● After reading Chapter 3, remind the children that letters were a more important means of communication when this book was written. Examine the railway children's letter. Ask: *In what ways have they tried to be formal?* (The proper form of a letter; division into complete sentences; careful punctuation.) Suggest that modern children might write a less formal note. How does the writer still emphasise the childishness of the letter-writers? (Some of their expressions; spelling mistakes; ideas.)

● Re-read Peter's encounter with the Station Master on the road. Discuss Peter's embarrassment and the Station Master's kindness.

● Consider how the Station Master is presented. (His speech is grammatically correct, unlike that of the servants and the cart man.) Agree that he is in a position of authority and responsibility and so is educated.

● Suggest that, after writing to the old gentleman, Peter decides to write to the Station Master. What does he want to say? (Further apologies; pleasure that they are now friends.)

● Ask the children to write two letters: one from Peter to the Station Master and one as his reply. Emphasise thinking about what to say, and how these characters express it.

> **Differentiation**
> **For older/more confident learners:** Ask children to write Mother's letter to the Station Master when she learns about the coal mining.
> **For younger/less confident learners:** Suggest content ideas and limit the letters' length.

Get writing

Newspaper views

> **Objective:** In non-narrative, establish, balance and maintain viewpoints.
> **What you need:** Copies of *The Railway Children*, writing materials.
> **Cross-curricular link:** Citizenship

What to do
● Use this activity after Chapter 8.
● Draw attention to the extended periods of free time that the railway children have. Hold partner, and then class, discussions about the advantages of this: independence; self-reliance; interesting happenings; involvement with their community. Talk about disadvantages: no formal education; potential danger; lack of adult guidance.
● Remind the children of the 9.14 train. Ask: *Are the passengers shocked that the three children are always available to wave to them and without adult supervision? Are they impressed by their independence?*

● Discuss the probable identity of many of these passengers: businessmen going to work in London. Point out that such people may write letters to their local newspapers.
● Suggest their newspaper has received so many letters about children's free time that it is writing an editorial about it. Show a newspaper editorial, pointing out features: clear standpoint; arguments supported with evidence; statistics; quotes. Explain that a newspaper editorial attempts to persuade readers to have the same view.
● Ask the children to plan and write this editorial for the next edition of their local newspaper.

> **Differentiation**
> **For older/more confident learners:** Ask children to write a second editorial, taking the opposing view.
> **For younger/less confident learners:** Provide a writing frame: 'introduction', 'arguments', 'reasons', 'summary'.

Father's diary

> **Objective:** To vary the pace and develop the viewpoint through the portrayal of action and selected detail.
> **What you need:** Copies of *The Railway Children*, photocopiable page 29, writing materials.
> **Cross-curricular link:** History

What to do
● After finishing Chapter 13, ask: *What hints does the old gentleman give about Father?* (He says something nice may happen and *I have hopes*.)
● With only one chapter remaining, express surprise that, although Father is central to the story's events (changed lifestyle and proximity to the railway), the reader has learned nothing about him since Chapter 1, apart from vague references such as these.
● Ask partners to exchange known facts about Father. Pool them as a class, re-reading Bobbie's newspaper discovery and Mother's explanation

in Chapter 10. (He is in prison. Letters found in his desk were used as evidence of spying. Charged with being a spy and traitor, he was tried, found guilty and sentenced to five years' penal servitude.)
● Set a scenario: the writer wants to let the reader have occasional news from Father. To avoid confusion, his pages will be written in the first person, as diary extracts, and placed between chapters.
● Hand out photocopiable page 29, asking children to write the extracts with appropriate language and style, and to consider their placement in the book.

> **Differentiation**
> **For older/more confident learners:** Ask children to research prison conditions of 1905.
> **For younger/less confident learners:** Encourage preliminary partner preparation and accept shorter pieces of writing.

Get writing

Story planning

> **Objective:** To reflect independently and critically on their own writing and edit and improve it.
> **What you need:** Copies of *The Railway Children*, photocopiable page 30, writing materials.
> **Cross-curricular link:** History.

What to do

● Express regret that *The Railway Children* has no sequel. (Compare Jill Murphy's *The Worst Witch* series.)

● Set a scenario: the children have been asked to write a sequel in keeping with the original book. Ask: *What should stay the same?* (The children; the style of writing; the railway's importance.) *What could change?* (The plot's adventures and mysteries.)

● Invite partners, then the class, to share ideas for a new *The Railway Children* book. Prompt by asking: *When is the story set?* (For example, in the school holidays.) *What is the mystery?*

(Luggage goes missing from the station.) *What is the adventure?* (A house is flooded.) *What do the railway children do?* (Find the luggage and make a rescue.) *What is the ending?* (Perks has his job back.)

● Consider a story's chronological structure: opening; incidents; complications; events to sort them out; ending. Talk about the value of subplots to keep readers interested.

● Give out photocopiable page 30. Invite the children to complete their plan with brief notes. Keep the plans for the next activity.

> **Differentiation**
> **For older/ more confident learners:** Suggest children add character notes on the back of the photocopiable sheet.
> **For younger/less confident learners:** Abbreviate the plan and let partners share plot ideas.

Becoming writers

> **Objective:** To set their own challenges to extend achievement and experience in writing.
> **What you need:** The children's completed story plans from the 'Story planning' activity, copies of *The Railway Children*, writing materials.
> **Cross-curricular link:** History.

What to do

● Remind the children of the previous activity: planning the plot of a sequel to *The Railway Children*. Remind them that they must match Nesbit's style.

● Re-read Chapter 10, which is typical of Nesbit's writing. Draw attention to paragraph length; detailed descriptions; abundant dialogue and Nesbit's careful application of direct-speech rules. (A new paragraph is started whenever someone starts or finishes speaking.) Point out emphasised spoken words (*forgetting, that, must*). Do they help the reader to 'hear' the speakers?

● Indicate the sentence *Praise helps people very*

much sometimes towards the end of Chapter 10. Is it a comment from the writer? Remind the children that Nesbit occasionally makes comments to the reader.

● Return the children's planning sheets from the previous activity. Let them remind themselves of their plans by using their notes to tell their story to a partner.

● Allocate time for writing the story, perhaps over the forthcoming weeks. Suggest the children consider a target length and add a time plan to their notes: how much they should write for each section and how long to spend writing it.

● Ask the children to begin writing their story.

> **Differentiation**
> **For older/more confident learners:** Encourage more ambitious targets and other aspects of Nesbit's style.
> **For younger/less confident learners:** Advise the children in setting realistic writing targets.

Mood poetry

● Imagine Mother is going to write a poem about the family moving house to make the children less anxious. Write your poem in the style of Mother's other poems.

Title: _____

They had a home that they loved
A place of joy and fun,

_____

_____

_____

_____

_____

_____

Illustrations © 2011, Mike Lacey, Beehive Illustration.

Father's diary

● Write four extracts from Father's diary. Decide which chapters to place each extract between.

Between Chapters _____ and _____

Between Chapters _____ and _____

Between Chapters _____ and _____

Between Chapters _____ and _____

Illustration © 2011, Mike Lacey, Beehive Illustration.

Get writing

Story planning

● Write your plan for a sequel to *The Railway Children* under the headings below.

Opening
Where? When? Who?

Incidents	
Mysteries	Adventures
1.	1.
2.	2.

Complications and dilemmas
Who has a difficult decision to make? What do they decide? What else goes wrong?

Resolution
How is the mystery solved? How does the adventure turn out?

Ending

Assessment

Assessment advice

This story's themes are layered. In the outer layer are the children's adventures and the adults' mysteries and secrets. Assess the children's grasp of these themes by arranging pairs to improvise the dialogue of two railway children discussing their adventures. Put yourself in the hot-seat as an adult character – Father, Mother, the old gentleman, the Russian gentleman or Perks. Invite the children to question you in order to uncover a mystery or secret. Their questions will reveal their understanding.

In the inner layer is the theme of moral justice. Justice can be a hazy concept, but E. Nesbit presents a clear view of right and wrong. The story's moral code propounds that good, correct behaviour will bring its own reward. Assess understanding by asking partners, in character as Peter, Phyllis or Mother, to cite an occasion when they did 'the right thing' and were rewarded in a non-material way.

Journeys are the spine of the story: the journey from town to country and Father's journey from unjust accusation to just freedom. Mother and the children also make a journey in courage, inventiveness and self-reliance. Use drama to assess awareness of this, naming a characteristic and a character and asking the children to mime an example. Can they explain it and suggest that character's likely behaviour in the first part of Chapter 1?

What does she think now?

> **Assessment focus:** To deduce, infer or interpret information, ideas or events from texts.
> **What you need:** Copies of *The Railway Children*, photocopiable page 32, writing materials.

What to do

● Focus the children's attention on Bobbie's place in the story. Suggest that Bobbie is the railway child who receives most attention and sympathy from the writer. The story traces her journey in the understanding of adult feelings and behaviour. Let the children work individually to assess their awareness of this development.

● Give photocopiable page 32 to each child. Ask them to find each situation in the story, read the relevant pages, enter Bobbie's head and write what she is thinking about each event. Less confident learners may provide notes and oral answers. The activity will allow you to check the children's understanding of the explicit plot and to assess their ability to deduce implicit information.

● Expect the children to give the following sorts of answers:

 ● I know from Mother's face that she does not want to laugh. She is being brave for us.

 ● I do not want praise. I cannot forget that people were nearly killed.

 ● Mother is exhausted. I must distract Phyllis so Mother can think quietly.

 ● I believe now that there is good in everyone as long as you are kind to them.

 ● I understand why Mother has not shared this terrible secret with us. I have to do the same and not tell Peter and Phyllis.

 ● I trust the old gentleman. There must be hope for Father or he would not have said this. I still cannot tell Mother.

What does she think now?

● Write how Bobbie is feeling at that time in each thought bubble.

Chapter 1: Mother laughs when Peter says he likes moving.

Chapter 13: Bobbie walks to the gate with the old gentleman.

Chapter 6: The children return home after stopping the train.

Chapter 11: Bobbie talks to Mother about what she has read in the newspaper.

Chapter 7: Bobbie challenges Phyllis to a race.

Chapter 8: Bobbie tells Mother about the Bargee's kindness.

Illustration © 2011, Mike Lacey, Beehive Illustration.